TWO-HOUR GARDEN ART

TWO-HOUR GARDEN ART

Ruby Begonia

Sterling Publishing Co., Inc. New York
A Sterling/Chapelle Book

Chapelle Ltd.

Owner:
Jo Packham

Editor:
Kristi Torsak

Writers:
Jo Packham, Wendy Toliver

Staff:
Areta Bingham, Kass Burchett,
Marilyn Goff, Holly Hollingsworth,
Susan Jorgensen, Barbara Milburn,
Linda Orton, Karmen Quinney,
Cindy Stoeckl, Kim Taylor, Sara Toliver

Photographers:
Kevin Dilley for Hazen Imaging Inc.,
Scot Zimmerman Photography,
Leslie M. Newman, Robert Perron,
Anita Louise Crane

Library of Congress Cataloging-in-Publication Data Available

10 9 8 7 6 5 4 3 2 1

Published by Sterling Publishing Company, Inc.,
387 Park Avenue South, New York, NY 10016
© 2001 by Ruby Begonia
Distributed in Canada by Sterling Publishing
c/o Canadian Manda Group, One Atlantic Avenue, Suite 105
Toronto, Ontario, Canada M6K 3E7
Distributed in Great Britain and Europe by Cassell PLC
Wellington House, 125 Strand, London WC2R 0BB, England
Distributed in Australia by Capricorn Link (Australia) Pty Ltd.
P.O. Box 6651, Baulkham Hills, Business Centre, NSW 2153, Australia

All Rights Reserved
Sterling ISBN 0-8069-4787-X   H

If you have any questions or comments, please contact:

Chapelle Ltd., Inc.
P. O. Box 9252
Ogden, UT 84409
(801) 621-2777 FAX (801) 621-2788
e-mail: Chapelle@chapelleltd.com
website: www.chapelleltd.com

Ruby & Begonia

As you walk down historic 25th Street in Ogden, Utah, the first thing you might notice is a copper sign surrounded by hand-forged copper flowers and garlands of crystals that glisten in the noonday sun. The sign reads, "Ruby & Begonia," and immediately you feel you must enter. As you walk through the etched glass doors, you feel as if you have walked into the home of someone you have known and loved for a very long time. The month of year you enter dictates what room of the home that you see first. Because the décor at Ruby & Begonia changes with the first day of each new month, you will probably be somewhat surprised each time you walk in.

If you enter on a crisp clear morning in April, you may walk right into grandmother's kitchen with Easter eggs being dyed on top of vintage tables. As you look around, you will see that all of the gift and décor items have been painted the pastel colors of Spring. If you enter on an afternoon in May when the smell of white lilacs is in the air, you may visit a lady's Victorian sitting room with a bed covered in deep down comforters and soft white coverlets, and lace-covered dressing tables with jewelry and niceties of all design arranged neatly atop. The cooler early evenings of November may, of course, lead you into a dining room with a warm glow from a welcoming fireplace and a large wooden table set for a family gathering and Thanksgiving dinner.

At Ruby & Begonia some of the items are vintage, while others are handcrafted by the country's finest artisans. All are unique, extraordinary, and appeal to the heart and soul of each who enters in a different and very personal way.

Ruby & Begonia, a retail outlet established at the beginning of the new millennium, is a store whose approach to retailing is as innovative, as conscious of the limitations of time and money, and as truly enjoyable as is *Two-Hour Garden Art*. It is the kind of place where you find ideas that are simple, creative, and can be merely temporary or that last an entire lifetime. *Two-Hour Garden Art* is Ruby & Begonia's first of many publications to come—each of which will teach you something new, reteach something old, and offer instructions on how to create something not only worth making, but worth keeping.

TABLE OF CONTENTS

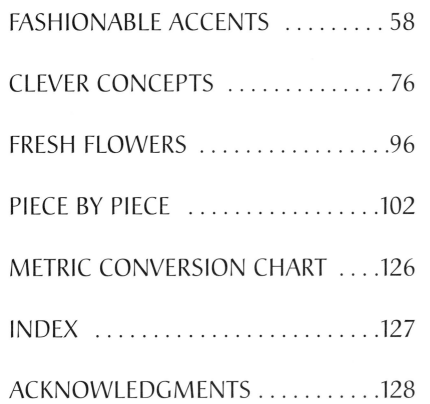

Foreword

Garden art can be something that is an obvious addition to porches, pathways, and gardens; or it can be an idea—a way of displaying a single item or decorating with your favorite collectibles. Garden art can be brought together in as little as two hours, or at two-hour intervals over a longer period of time. Adding garden art to your natural surroundings doesn't mean you have to stay with what is traditional or permanent. Look at the photographs that follow and use your imagination. Use the same energy when decorating the outside of your home that you would when decorating the living room or kitchen. The out-of-doors is simply another ideal place to add your personal touch.

$\mathcal{I}$ntroduction

The desire to add "art" and "ornamentation" to our daily lives is as ancient as man and civilization itself. To weave patterns in the cloth that covers our bodies or in the baskets in which we carry the necessities of life; or to paint figures upon the walls of the caves and to embellish our architecture is as natural as draping our necks with brilliant beads of shells or cloaking our shoulders with feathers and fur. To add a simple or an ornate touch of art to ourselves or our environment is that which sets each individual apart, establishes a social standing, and enriches one's surroundings.

Even in our gardens, bedecked with nature's finest fruits and flowers, the desire to add ornaments is hard to resist. Ancient man placed sundials in the heart of his fields. During the Victorian era, men added immense statues and trimmed their hedges in precise designs. In today's world, one gardener hangs handmade wooden birdhouses from the limbs of an apple tree, one builds ornamental fences around an herb garden, while another fills unusual birdbaths with colored rocks and fancy pedestals for feathered friends. No matter the century in which we live or the land in which we dwell, all gardeners are compelled to place their stamp upon their gardens and add their own human artistic touch to nature's many glories.

We dress up and domesticate our gardens in other ways, of course, with garden gates, whitewashed fences and vintage furniture, as well as painted garden walls, trimmed hedges, small statuary, and decorative garden lights. Such additions bring structure to a garden space and help to define its mood and uses. It is these ornaments that season the garden with individual taste and nuances of flavor, and that delight us or set us to contemplation. Whether the ornament is fine art, folk art, or born of pure utility, whether it is steeped in tradition or has never been used in garden settings before, it delights the eye, brings peace to an individual's soul, becomes the gardener's voice, and undeniably establishes the gardener's presence.

The most important element in adding art to your garden is: what art causes you to feel each time you enter or leave your garden.

To each gardener, the concept of ornament and art is as different as the reasons for which one becomes a gardener. To some it is the fruits left from the necessities of substance for the family dinner table. To some it is rigid defined lines that are needed to help stabilize a chaotic world; to some it is grandeur that adds elegance to an ordinary predictable life-style; and to others it is simplicity to help balance an overabundance of information and communication.

The reasons for adding art to your garden are as natural and as varied as the days of the year. What matters most is not the why but the result and the meaning to you, the gardener.

Home fronts

Whether walking from the road to the house or from the house to the road, the visitor's attention often focuses on the front porch. After all, one of the glories of any gardener and garden is a place for relaxation where one can find a simple peace. What better place to relax, to welcome, or to bid farewell than the porch?

Front porches have been an important architectural element in home design for over 200 years. It is the transitional space between what was once considered the prim and proper indoors and the beauty of the outside world.

The architectural style of each home should dictate the style and décor of the porch. In addition, the porch, the furniture, and the art it exhibits should be in sync with the inhabitant's life-style and purposes for which they wish the porch to serve.

Garden art can be added to a porch in a matter of moments. The porches pictured here are ones that are more casual and country in nature. They are furnished with natural pieces that assimilate nicely into the surrounding environment and homeowners' life-styles. The pieces are well worn and much used. Nonetheless, these porches can be either feminine or masculine, expected or a slight contradiction, vintage or somewhat country contemporary. It is the attention to the small details, which can be accomplished in minutes, that adds a unique style to garden art.

On this old-fashioned southern porch, planters secured at an angle on the railing offer a slight relief from the straight, formal guidelines adhered to by southern gentility.

Baskets of like flowers that match the color of the porch's walls and flooring, a tiny heart chain, and matching chairs are all pieces of garden art.

Victorian porches are often quite feminine in their decoration and are places where new art is added sometimes on a daily basis. For a lover of Victorian finery, there is always room to add one more delicate touch. These porches are graceful and romantic, and are charming places to share memories with old friends.

Items placed on such a porch can be vintage in nature or newly handmade. Layers of lace, yards of fabric, mismatched pieces of china, chairs angled just right for a tête-à-tête and a cup of tea, decorations and furnishings typically seen indoors—all help create the perfect setting for the summer sunshine to dance over the conversation of good friends.

Traditional Victorian porches are usually covered, allowing such scenes to be set and left from day to day. They are not put away as the evening sun sets—for they must be ready for early morning callers.

In the photographs here, lace and floral linens adorn tables of all shapes and sizes, mimicking the elegant floral arrangements used as centerpieces and rail trimmings. Straw baskets, sunhats, and wicker furniture summon rays of sunlight and evoke a sense of airiness. Undoubtedly, anyone coming to such a porch will want to stay awhile to enjoy the time spent with friends, the herbal teas and homemade biscuits, and the generous cushions in the chairs—all of which guarantee a comfortable afternoon.

In the true shabby-chic spirit, this porch spins trinkets from the past into treasures of today. A whimsical concoction of beauty, comfort, and usefulness, the shabby-chic porch spurs imaginative and lively conversation.

In these photographs, many of the decorations were found in flea markets, antique shops, and estate and garage sales. Worn and used chairs and couches are delightfully mismatched. Contemporary and unexpected, a dress ornamented with beads and silk flowers was made by the artisan who lives here. On special occasions, weather permitting, she hangs it daintily in her garden for friends and family to enjoy. A tile-topped table offers a place to set a tray of cocktails or a favorite family board game. Spherical Japanese-style lanterns strung along strings of twinkling outdoor lights bring the moon and stars down to earth for an evening of festivities.

Grapevines grow over and around this porch from only a few small vines planted one evening by friends. The grapes are often picked to serve to guests.

One of the advantages to a shabby-chic style of art is that it can be accumulated over time with no worries of pieces matching or being too worn. Here, peeling paint, faded cushions, or a table with missing tiles adds to the style, the charm, and the ease of maintaining such a place.

Paper lanterns can be used anywhere—on the porch or in the garden—that a party mood is wanted. Just be certain to use outdoor decorative lights and take the paper lanterns in before retiring if the porch is not covered. Rain, wind, and sun will ruin such décor if they are left outside.

Hanging baskets, whether on the porch or in the garden, whether conventional or innovative, display flowers and other plants so they are readily noticed and appreciated. The baskets or containers holding the flowers or the greenery are easy to make and to plant. There are literally hundreds of publications available to teach a new or an experienced gardener how to create these and what to plant, depending on the location and the weather conditions of where you live. The basket or container can be practically invisible, highly decorative, and anything in between. The only prerequisites are that it holds the plant securely and allows excess water to escape.

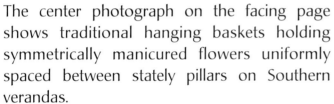

The center photograph on the facing page shows traditional hanging baskets holding symmetrically manicured flowers uniformly spaced between stately pillars on Southern verandas.

More nontraditional hanging baskets are pictured on this page. Securing familiar baskets to the outside of the house, a fence, or a gate is an unexpected addition of garden art. The copper pot is attached with an iron hanger to a painted wall plaque, then hung on a fence.

The terra-cotta pots to the right are painted, decoupaged following manufacturer's instructions, and hung with a simple linked chain from this tree.

Point of view

When windows are adorned with flowers and foliage, nature and the indoors are separated merely by a pane of glass. The top-left photograph shows how vines can transform into custom outdoor drapes that are as beautiful from the inside as they are the outside. Planter boxes can be arranged underneath windows, and the showcased plants can be rotated to reflect a mood, an occasion, or a season. Small vintage pieces can be quietly positioned in a display of flowers for additional interest, and ideas can be taken from retail establishments to use on your home. Bright colors, large lettering, and an overabundance of flowers would make any window beautiful. When windows are decorated like these, both passersby and the people living within enjoy their beauty.

23

project
WINDOW
SHELF

A window shelf can be customized to fit the gardener's personal style. Paint it a color that coordinates with the house, or use bright bold contrasting colors. Choose an antique wooden trim, or opt for a modern design detail. When the shelf is hung, the plants can be in matching pots or pots of varying sizes, colors, and shapes. Perhaps the plants are not planted in pots at all. Consider using old bowls, discarded kitchen pots and pans, or a variety of metal milk pitchers. Just make certain whatever you use has a drainage hole.

Instructions

1. Secure finials and decorative edging to bottom of shelf with screws.

2. Paint shelf with desired color and let dry.

3. Hang shelf below desired window with brackets and screws.

Materials	_Supplies_
Brackets	Paintbrush
Decorative wooden edging	Screwdriver
Exterior paint, desired color	
Screws	
Wooden finials	
Wooden shelf	

The shelf at the right on the outside of the window can be as inviting as shelves on the inside. They need not simply hold pots of plants, but can offer refreshment for those who are visiting or working in the garden. Fresh oranges or apples in a basket that can withstand the elements and a corked pottery jug of fresh water or lemonade gives a European flavor of hospitality to a traditional American home and neighborhood.

Window ledges, such as the one pictured below, need not be fancy or overdone to be appealing or enchanting. Simple flowers in traditional pots can bring just the right amount of color and design for an afternoon party or an entire season.

The advantage of using such effortless decorating is that it appeals to more than one type of decorator. To some, anything more would be overdone, and to others who weary of the same thing day after day, the pots and the plants they contain can be easily changed as often as desired.

Even though this display is modest, the idea offers an unlimited number of possibilities. The plants can be the same type and color or each can be different. Each pot can be an exact duplicate or each can be as different as the flowers they contain.

When windows are adorned with flowers or foliage, curtains or banners, knickknacks or fancy fretwork, nature and the indoors are separated merely by a pane of glass. The indoors and the outdoors are in such close proximity, it is almost as if they are one. Do not forget that on the outside of the house the windows become a major focal point for all who are looking in their direction. They should be as interesting and decorated with art as the porch or garden.

The window on the facing page has a small quilt that offers privacy to those on the inside, yet allows those on the outside to feel as if they are part of the inside of the home. Since this quilt was not made to be admired from both sides, the homeowner hand-stitched another small quilt to the reverse side.

Upper right: Sheer lace curtains and favored mementos give a sense to the passerby of the type of people that dwell on the inside of this home. These pieces are fun for all to examine from both inside and outside the home. They can create a mood simply because they evoke memories of the time they were purchased, or the era in which they were valued. Arrange them, rearrange them, change them—everyone will enjoy the newness of each collection.

Lower right: Ordinary windows can be quickly changed to extraordinary by a coat of richly colored paint and small pieces of fretwork nailed just inside the window trim. A row of daylilies is planted underneath in colors that not only complement but call attention to this very special piece of garden art.

*C*reative outdoors

Outdoor garden art should fit the needs of those who design it, build it, and enjoy it. It need not be traditional or simply for enjoyment. It can be something that is built for an intended temporary purpose.

The story of this neighborhood lemonade stand is one that is worth repeating. Not only did it serve the purpose for which it was constructed, it also added color, flavor, and flair to the garden in which it was built. It was a piece of garden art that was enjoyed by everyone who lived close by or just happened to visit. It was a delight to see and participate in.

project
LEMONADE STAND

Materials
Banner (see Instructions for
Banner on page 32)
Canvas fabric
Children's artwork
Cinder blocks
(as many as needed)
Cloth tape (e.g. duct tape)
Exterior paints, desired colors
Flags and/or signs
Nails
PVC® pipes 48"–60"
Sturdy platform or
base for table(s)
Table(s)
Umbrellas
Yard art

Supplies
Craft scissors
Hammer
Paintbrushes
(as many as needed)
Tape measure

Note: Lemonade stand shown was set on a 4"-high platform over the street curb and supported with cinder blocks. The platform was built from plywood and 2x4s. The artwork in these photographs was created and drawn by children.

Instructions

1. Position and level sturdy platform that will support weight of table(s) and children. Paint platform with desired color and let dry.

2. Measure and cut canvas to fit around platform.

3. Paint canvas with desired colors and pattern. Let dry.

4. Secure canvas to platform with nails to create stand.

5. Paint table(s) with desired color(s) and let dry.

6. Position table(s) on stand. Tape banners and artwork to table(s) and canvas.

7. Attach umbrellas to stand for shade. Place PVC pipe(s) into cinder blocks and push against platform. Attach flags and/or signs.

8. Paint yard art to match stand and let dry. Position around stand for a decorative effect.

There are lessons to be learned from everyone with whom we come in contact; and just such a lesson was taught by the creator and the participants of this delightful project.

Amy Adams is an art professor at Weber State University in Ogden, Utah. She lives in an older neighborhood in the city with her husband and her adopted animals. Amy is a member of an organization that was created for the purpose of supporting and protecting homeless or injured animals.

When summer vacation rolled around the younger children in Amy's neighborhood did not have enough to do to fill the long sunny afternoons. Amy was busy working for a local animal shelter and needed some help to raise money. It occurred to her that she and the children in the neighborhood could build a lemonade stand, sell lemonade, cookies, and dog biscuits, and give the money to the organization. It would give the children something positive to do with their days and it would help Amy; but most of all, it would help the animals.

Amy and the children began their endeavor by building their stand in Amy's front yard. It was constructed so that it was off of the street, and the children and their customers were in no danger. Amy and her coworkers began frequenting garage sales in the neighborhood to find the "perfect" items to decorate their new establishment. They even collected lanterns and Christmas lights so that passersby could see the result of their efforts in the late evening hours. After all, if they were going to have people stop, they had to get their attention. To further stimulate outside interest, signs were designed by the children, printed, and hung on telephone poles throughout the neighborhood.

The children each drew artwork for the stand. They had logo art, banner art, art for visors, fans, flyers, and jewelry. They decided the animals needed a patron saint so the lemonade stand served a purpose; so each participant drew an image of what their saint may look like.

The children worked together to decorate the stand and create the items to be sold. They even devised a work schedule so that someone would be working at the stand at the busiest times of the day and the responsibilities would be divided evenly among the group.

The banners were so colorful, the decorations were so inviting, and the enthusiasm was so contagious that the stand was busier than they had hoped. The local newspaper heard about their establishment and their goals and wrote a full-page article in support of the animal shelter, the children, and their lemonade stand.

The lemonade and cookies were the perfect refreshment for hot Utah summer days, and the other items for sale were irresistible. The fans pictured above were made by one of the children. Favorite pet pictures were cut from magazines, scanned into the computer, and then printed on card stock. The image was cut into the shape of a fan, mounted on a piece of poster board and a brightly painted stick (designed originally for stirring paint) was glued to the back. The fans were as welcome in the heat of the sun as were the glasses of lemonade and ice water.

Of course, all of the neighborhood dogs were welcome to spend an afternoon with the kids. What better way to attract supporters of the animal shelter than with dogs and dog biscuits? The project was a success, and the children and neighbors learned a great deal from their creative endeavor.

The banner above was designed by the children who were such an important part of this summer project. It is a wonderful piece of garden art that is not usually considered by most to be an addition that one would want in their garden. It was, however, colorful, inviting, and designed to resist the elements. It served its purpose of decorating a section of a garden that needed to be designed to get attention and attract passersby.

BANNER

Materials	Supplies
Acrylic paints, desired colors	Grommet installer
Canvas 18" x 48"	Paintbrushes
Grommets (4–5)	(as many as needed)
Rope	

Instructions

1. Lay canvas on clean, flat surface. Have children paint name, logo, and any decorative elements on canvas with desired colors to create banner.

2. Let dry 24 hours.

3. Insert grommets into banner, following manufacturer's directions. Position them as follows: one in each corner and one in center of each long edge for stability.

4. Hang by threading rope through grommets in corners and anchoring with rope in center grommets.

The children put a great deal of thought into the items that they sold. They knew their most popular ideas would be those that were useful on hot summer days—lemonade, ice water, fans, and visors. Some of the initial monies earned from the sale of lemonade purchased plain visors. Not only were the visors big sellers, they were used by the daily workers and offered additional color and interest to the stand. They had the same effect as hanging ornaments on a Christmas tree.

project

VISOR LABELS

Materials
Colored alligator clips
Self-adhesive printer labels
Visors

Supplies
Computer (optional)
Markers (optional)
Printer (optional)

Instructions

1. Have children write name and logo of lemonade stand on labels; or print information for stand onto labels with computer and printer.

2. Stick labels onto front of visor.

3. Using clips, hang visors from umbrellas on lemonade stand.

project
NECKLACE

Materials
Nylon thread
Plastic beads and charms
Potato
Spray paint, desired color(s)

Supplies
Needle
Potato peeler
Sharp knife

Instructions

1. Peel potato and dice into small squares.

2. Using needle, string diced potato pieces onto nylon thread. Hang by thread tightly or lay flat, and space pieces approximately ½" apart to air-dry.

3. When dry, unstring potato pieces and spray-paint, following manufacturer's directions. Let dry.

4. Using needle, string potato pieces onto nylon thread along with plastic charms and beads. Tie ends together with a double knot to secure.

Lemonade Recipe

Ingredients:
12 lemons
2 limes
2 oranges
3 quarts water
1½–2 cups sugar

Directions:
Squeeze juice from lemons, limes, and oranges. Pour into container. Add sugar and water to juices; mix well. Store in refrigerator. Serve with ice.

Sugar Cookie Recipe

Ingredients:
1½ cups powdered sugar
1 cup shortening
1 egg
1½ teaspoons vanilla extract
2½ cups flour
1 teaspoon baking soda
1 teaspoon cream of tartar

Directions:
Preheat oven to 350° F. Lightly grease cookie sheet. Mix sugar, shortening, egg, and vanilla until creamy. Mix in flour, baking soda, and cream of tartar. Make several small balls of dough. Roll out dough to approximately ¼" thick. Cut into desired shapes with cookie cutters. Place cookies onto cookie sheet and bake for 8–10 minutes.

Inspirational winter

Gardens should not only be beautiful if adorned for spring and summer, they should also offer ideas of inspiration to all who visit or pass by during every season of the year. Even without the colorful flowers and green grass, a garden can still be aesthetically pleasing—even beautiful—in the winter. Fences, gates, vases, pots, and planters look so pristine when snowcapped. Add frost and icicles to the scene, and the picture is one of a winter wonderland. The fence pictured here is made from old gates, table legs, balusters, and headboards—all salvaged from thrift stores and garage sales. In the spring, the bedposts are used as trellises for climbing roses. Hydrangea bushes plant-ed behind the "posts" add color. There is even an old hanging lamp secured between balusters where a candle is placed on calm evenings.

To construct a fence similar to this, measure the length for the fence placement and divide the space evenly to determine the location of the supporting 4x4 posts. Set 4x4s 24 inches deep in concrete at regular intervals. If the spans are too long, additional ground supports can be added by putting 4x4s on either side of the fixed posts, with cross-Ts cut to fit between and hold the decorative elements in place. Stretch a level line between the posts and cut 2x4s to the desired height. Place additional 2x4s between posts to support the top rail, in case any of the decorative elements do not reach the height of the top rail. Attach all of the pieces of the fence together with wood screws and lag bolts. Make every effort to eliminate the appearance of connecting devices.

During the fresh days of spring, the sun-drenched summer afternoons, and the cool fall evenings—when the garden is beginning, at its peak, or coming to a close—garden art for the most part plays only a supporting role. However, during the months of winter, it is ornament that commands the stage. Its presence lends a certain beauty to the barren trees, the garden walks, and the empty flower beds.

Upper left: Hanging outdoor lanterns are oftentimes more beautiful during the winter months than they are in summer. The days of winter are so much shorter, the nights so much longer, that tiny burning candles hanging from the trees offer a greeting of welcome to visitors and passersby.

These hanging candleholders are made from old Mexican wrought-iron lamps that were found in a thrift store. The colored glass and electrical workings were removed from the inside of the lamps. Chains were added to create lanterns that could be hung from hooks on the limbs of the trees. The candles are placed in the lanterns just before lighting. If left in the elements unlit, the wick becomes frozen and ice puddles in the melted core of the candle.

Lower left: This large iron garden urn is left outside during the winter months to be filled with snow. Just before the holiday season, a tiny Christmas tree is planted and decorated. During the summer months, it sometimes contains potted plants, or sometimes a collection of seashells. During the months of fall, pinecones can be found spilling over the top. Regardless of the season, it is a beautiful addition of garden art to the front porch of this old brick home.

Window shelves can be used during the winter months for a variety of reasons. Here, left empty, they exhibit a beautiful display of mounded snow and hanging icicles. During the holidays, they hold pots with tiny evergreen trees and miniature bushes of holly. It is also during the winter months that these shelves receive their patina finish. The copper covering, left to weather, turns a beautiful color of teal green after the snow has fallen and the ice has melted.

The copper theme is continued on the side of this beautiful brick home by hanging copper trellises on either side of the window. During spring, summer, and fall, climbing vines accentuate the potted plants placed on the shelf top.

This shelf is made in much the same manner as the copper tabletop shown on page 40. A standard wooden shelf was covered with squares of copper, which were overlapped slightly and nailed in place. On the front of the shelf, green glass drawer pulls were screwed in and secured. These will be used for hanging pots and wind chimes during the summer months. The shelf is supported by ornate metal shelf brackets that will rust during the winter months, to match the rusted trellises on each side of the shelf.

Copper tabletops and planters are perfect for outdoor use through every season. The patina finish that is acquired after months of snow, rain, and sun is more beautiful to some than the sheen of the original copper. However, if you prefer that the copper does not age, there are clear coatings that can be easily applied several times during the seasons to prevent the copper color turning to verdigris.

Copper containers are placed on this table all winter long to bring added interest to the patio. During the spring, the first blossoms are potted and placed where all can see and flowering plants are placed between the green shrubs. These containers are a year-round addition to any garden. The planter on the facing page is planted with small shrubs that stay green even in the winter months.

Instructions

1. Cut copper sheeting into geometric shapes such as squares or triangles.

2. Position copper shapes on table in desired pattern, overlapping each other slightly and leaving ½" overlap on table edge. (Shown is a crazy-quilt pattern.)

3. Predrill holes ¼" deep through copper shapes and into table.

4. Nail copper shapes to table to create copper tabletop.

5. Trim copper tabletop to ³⁄₁₆" around table edges and file to smooth.

6. Bend and hammer copper tabletop down over table edges.

project
COPPER
TABLETOP
(photograph on facing page)

Materials	Supplies
Copper sheeting	Drill and bit
Copper weather-	Hammer
stripping nails	Metal file
Table	Metal shears

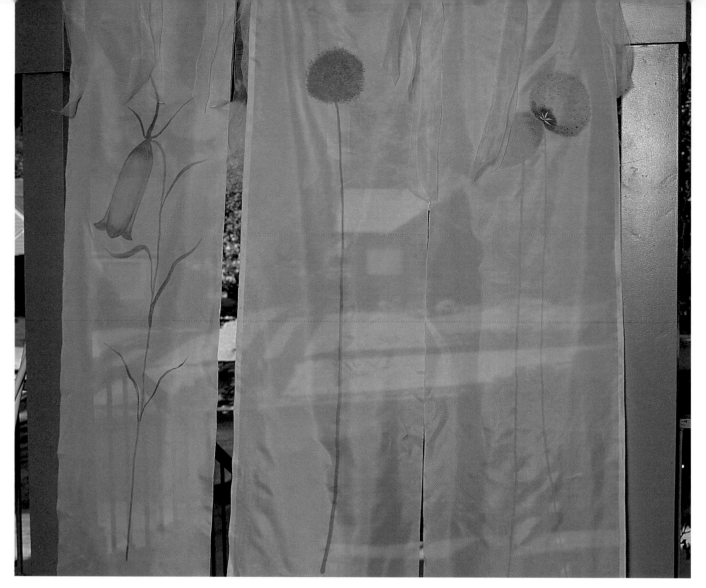

project
PATIO
SHEERS

Materials
Acrylic paints:
pink, purple, teal
Fabric medium
Fray preventative
Sheer curtain panels
40" x 84" (2)
Sheer ribbon 2"-wide,
coordinating color
Thread, coordinating color

Supplies
Fabric scissors
Needle
Paintbrush
Sponge
Tape measure

Instructions

1. Cut each panel in half lengthwise. Apply fray preventative to cut edges.

2. Mix paint with fabric medium, following manufacturer's directions.

3. Lay panels flat on protected surface. Sponge and/or paint desired pattern and let dry. (Shown are floral patterns.)

4. Cut ribbon into 24" lengths, three per panel.

5. Fold ribbon in half. Using needle and thread, attach ribbon fold to top of panel at top left, top center, and top right. Repeat for all panels.

Facing page: Just because the bears are hibernating doesn't mean everyone must stay indoors. A sunny winter afternoon is a perfect opportunity to watch birds frolicking around the bird feeder. Slip on a fuzzy sweater and mittens, grab a favorite blanket and a mug of homemade hot cocoa, and relax on the back porch swing. If you need a little extra privacy and a little protection from the winter wind, but still want the light of the winter sun, hang sheers around the exposed side of the porch. It is amazing how quiet and peaceful the world becomes when covered in a blanket of freshly fallen snow.

This page: These plant holders are a surprising and delightful addition to any garden décor during any month. Made from discarded floor lamps, they can offer an endless number of possibilities for designing. Depending on the initial configuration of the lamp, they can be constructed in a wide variety of ways. They can be painted with bright or subtle colors, left plain, or have crystals attached. They can be used to hold candles for garden parties, fresh flower bouquets for weddings, or simply for the displaying of spring and summer blooming flowers. They are inexpensive, easy to construct (see *Lamp Planter instructions on pages 44–45*), and an unusual art piece that not everyone in the neighborhood already has.

project
LAMP
PLANTER

Materials
Coupler(s)
Floor lamp
Hex nuts
Metal chandelier
Nipple extensions
Plants
Potting soil
Spray paint, desired color
Terra-cotta pots: 4" (one
for each chandelier arm),
10" (for center if desired),
18" (for base)
Washers

Supplies
Needle-nosed pliers
Wire cutters

How to Disassemble Floor Lamp

1. Make certain lamp is not plugged into electrical outlet.

2. Unscrew top portion of floor lamp that holds light bulb to separate from pole. Discard top portion of lamp.

3. Using wire cutters, cut off electrical cord at base of floor lamp. Turn lamp upside down and pull electrical cord out through bottom of lamp.

How to Disassemble Chandelier

1. Make certain chandelier is not plugged into electrical outlet.

2. Unscrew finial on top or bottom of chandelier to get to center of electrical works. Using wire cutters, cut off electrical cord. (Note: Each chandelier arm has a light socket. Some can be turned to the left to remove and cut electrical cord. Others have a screw inside socket that must be removed for electrical cord to be cut; and still others have a finial on bottom of arm that, when removed, light socket will be loose and electrical cord can be cut.)

3. Pull out all electrical wires from arms and center of chandelier.

How to Attach Center Pot

Note: If the pole of floor lamp being used is screwed together in the center, a pot can be added.

1. Disassemble lamp, following How to Disassemble Floor Lamp directions.

2. Enlarge drainage hole in pot to accommodate threaded rod of floor lamp. (Note: If extra length is needed to add a pot, add a coupler and a nipple extension first to threaded rod.)

3. Place washer and then pot on threaded rod. Screw pole back together with pot in center.

Instructions

1. Disassemble lamp and discard all electrical parts, following How to Disassemble Floor Lamp directions.

2. Disassemble chandelier and discard all electrical parts, following How to Disassemble Chandelier directions.

3. Place chandelier over threaded rod of floor lamp and secure tightly with washer and hex nut to create lamp planter. (Note: If extra height is needed, add a coupler and a nipple extension first to threaded rod of floor lamp. Place chandelier over top of extension.)

4. Spray-paint entire lamp planter with two coats of desired color, following manufacturer's directions. Let dry 24 hours.

5. Fasten clay pot to chandelier arm with washer and hex nut. (Note: If extra length is needed to add pot, add a coupler and a nipple extension first to threaded rod of chandelier arm.) Repeat for all chandelier arms.

6. Place lamp base in large clay pot to create planter base. Cover lamp base with rocks to weight down for stability. (Note: If lamp base does not fit in bottom of pot, fill pot with rocks until base fits inside diameter of pot and cover lamp base with more rocks to weight down for stability.)

7. Fill planter base with soil and desired plants.

Sometimes a simple arrangement is all that is needed in the outside entryway to your home. Other times you may need just a little bit more. Here, a collection of treasures gathered from garden stores and salvage shops accents the area around the front door. A vintage newel post stands in the corner to add weight and a sense of strength to the collection. The statue of Francis of Asisis, the Patron Saint for animals is, of course, placed in a position of importance where he can watch over all. During the evening hours, metal urns and wire-mesh Chinese lanterns hold pillar candles to help light the way. If your front entry is covered from the rain and the snow, many objects can be placed to adorn the front of your home and welcome family and friends. Try bringing some of the pieces from inside the house, outside.

For those who like to trim the house for the holidays, it is just as much fun to decorate the outside as it is the inside. This summer porch has been turned into the perfect "living room" for this family Christmas tree and holiday celebration.

The tree was secured to the porch with wires tied around the trunk, then tied to posts on the porch. It was then decorated just like an inside tree with lights, ornaments, and beaded garlands. To secure the decorations, thin wire was used to wrap around and attach the individual pieces to the tree limbs. Unbreakable silver and gold balls were used to fill the Victorian hanging planters, and outdoor miniature lights were wrapped with crystal garlands and strung around the porch.

At intervals around the porch, individual sections of old hanging lights were hung and candles were added where the electrical fixtures once were. A festive opulent chandelier, found in a thrift store, was wired in place of the traditional porch light for the holidays. Tall candleholders were sprayed gold, draped with hanging crystals (also from a broken chandelier), and placed up the stairs to light the way.

Even the light in the center of the table to the lower right is one of those old hanging lights that were so popular in the '50s and '60s. It looks entirely different after having the chain removed and replacing the light bulbs with taper candles. When making such a piece, you must be careful that the top does not overheat while the candles are burning and that one piece of glass can be removed so that the candles can have enough air and be easily removed and replaced.

project
CRYSTAL TREE

Materials	*Supplies*
19-gauge wire	Tape measure
22-gauge wire	Wire cutters
Crystal bead strands	
approximately 46" long	
Gold spray paint	
Iron tree frame	

Note: The tree frame shown was constructed to specifications by a local professional welder.

Instructions

1. Spray-paint tree frame, following manufacturer's directions. Let dry 24 hours.

2. Measure crystal bead strands long enough to extend length of tree frame rods and cut (shown are 46" long). Wire two strands together with 19-gauge wire if extra length is needed.

3. Secure a strand of crystals to top of tree frame with 19-gauge wire.

4. Lay a strand of crystals flat on rod. Wrap 22-gauge wire around rod and strand between crystals, down length of rod.

5. Secure strand of crystals to bottom of tree frame with 19-gauge wire.

The crystal garlands that hung from the limbs of the tree were purchased at a flea market and are actually those that are used on chandeliers. The snowflake ornaments were made by soldering together four pieces of 20-gauge wire and adding beads to each section.

The crystal trees on the facing page can be hung on the wall, stand individually, or be wired back-to-back to make a more traditional tree shape. They can be used inside or out during the entire winter season. These were fashioned after a pair of Victorian crystal decorations that the owner saw in a magazine on Victorian homes and decorating.

49

Whims of summer

Sometimes spring starts slowly and ends far too soon, other times it seems as if it is missed altogether. However, when the lilacs have finished blooming and the tulips have dropped their petals, the gardener's porch and flower beds begin to show the true colors, smells, and traditional signs of summer.

It is during this time of the year that preparations are made for outdoor entertaining and parties, flowers are trimmed to encourage additional blooms, and care is taken to protect all that is fragile from the heat of the afternoon sun. These are the months when all inside work is put on hold until the nights are shorter and the weather is much colder; and for a short period, being outside is all that seems important. Working in the garden, decorating the porch with flowers, planting and repotting—nothing seems to be considered too much because the results are breathtaking, priceless, and fleeting.

project
DECOUPAGE
BUCKET

Materials
Antiquing medium
Decoupage medium
Galvanized bucket
Spray paint, desired color
Spray varnish
Wallpaper or
wrapping paper

Supplies
Clean dishcloths
Craft scissors
Paper towels
Sponge brush
Vinegar

Instructions

1. Wash bucket with vinegar and dishcloth. Dry with paper towels.

2. Spray-paint bucket, following manufacturer's directions. Let dry 24 hours.

3. Cut desired motifs from wallpaper or wrapping paper.

4. Using sponge brush, apply decoupage medium to bucket. Position one motif on bucket and smooth out any wrinkles or air bubbles with fingers. Position another motif on bucket and overlap as desired.

5. Using sponge brush, apply decoupage medium over motifs. Let dry until decoupage medium is no longer tacky.

6. Apply decoupage medium over entire bucket. Let dry 24 hours.

7. Apply antiquing medium, following manufacturer's directions. Using clean dishcloth, remove excess antiquing medium. Let dry.

8. Spray bucket with varnish, following manufacturer's directions.

The tradition of planting in pots is updated with these beautifully yet easily decoupaged garden buckets. The floral designs selected here imitate the flowers planted inside, but the paper that is used can be of any design or style. These details in the garden can be used outside during the months of summer and then taken indoors to be enjoyed during the colder months of winter. If the plants that are placed inside each pot are self-contained in clay pots, then on special occasions some of the buckets can have the plants removed and be used as ice buckets to hold bottles of wine, or soda pop.

Decoupage is an art form that can be done by almost anyone in a relatively short period of time. There is little or no skill involved, so there are few excuses not to decoupage anything and everything. To make it as quick and easy as possible, there are decoupage papers available that need little or no cutting. Cards, stickers, pieces of lace, or fabric can all be used to decorate the sides or tops of dinner ware, cans, chairs, tables, and any other décor you can imagine. Another nice thing about decoupage is that it is as permanent as almost any other art medium. The decoupage medium is fairly resistant to heat and water, and with a little common sense, objects can last for many seasons and be used for any number of reasons.

project
RUSTIC GARDEN ART

Materials	*Supplies*
Acrylic paints: metallic gold, blue-green, metallic pewter, rust, white	Bucket
	Craft sticks
	Disposable cup
Ceramic bird on steel post	Disposable plate
Desired plants	Eyedropper
Extrafine sand	Flat paintbrush 1"
Matte finish decoupage medium	Liquid dish soap
Potting soil	Medium-grit sandpaper
Quick-setting cement (1 bag)	Newspaper
Terra-cotta pots: 12", 14"	Paper towels
Two-step rusting agent	Rubbing alcohol
	Stirring stick

Instructions

1. Using plenty of newspaper, cover work surface to protect from runs and drips.

2. Clean surfaces of bird and pots with dish soap in tub of hot water. Let dry.

3. Using paper towel soaked with rubbing alcohol, wipe outer surface of bird and pots, making certain to clean all crevices and detailed areas. Let dry.

4. Sand bird and pots. Using paper towel soaked with rubbing alcohol, wipe bird and pots.

5. Using craft stick and disposable cup, mix two parts decoupage medium with one part water. Mix well.

6. Paint bird and pots with mixture for primer. Let dry.

7. Using craft stick and disposable cup, mix ¼ cup sand, one tablespoon decoupage medium, and two tablespoons white paint. Mix well.

8. Paint one coat of mixture over surfaces to be rusted.

9. Using craft stick and disposable plate, mix equal parts metallic gold and metallic pewter paints. Mix well.

10. Working vertically, paint with mixture over textured surfaces.

11. Paint streaks over metallic paint, before it dries, with blue-green and rust paints. Let dry.

12. Using eyedropper, apply two-step rusting agent to bird and pots, following manufacturer's directions. Let dry 24 hours.

13. Plug holes in bottom of terra-cotta pots and fill with water. Let soak for several hours.

14. Mix cement in bucket and stir, following manufacturer's directions. Empty water from pots.

15. Fill largest pot ⅓ to ½ full with cement. Set smaller pot inside and press down to adjust height.

16. Fill smaller pot ⅓ to ½ full with cement and stand post of rusted bird in cement. Hold in place until cement sets (approximately 10 minutes).

17. Allow cement to set up completely, following manufacturer's directions.

18. Fill pots with soil and desired plants.

project
PILLAR CANDLE- HOLDERS

Materials	*Supplies*
Baluster approximately 4" square	Dowel ½" diameter (optional)
Candles (3)	Hammer
Nails	Metal shears
Rusted tin	Paintbrush
White acrylic paint	Sandpaper
Wood glue	Saw
Wood screws	Screwdriver
Wooden 4x4s (2)	
Wooden boards 9" x 9" x 2" (3)	

Note: The rusted tin flowers shown were secured by drilling a hole in the top center of a candleholder and inserting tin stems into hole.

Instructions

1. Saw 4x4s to desired lengths for candleholders.

2. Paint all wooden pieces white and let dry.

3. Using sandpaper, distress wooden pieces for desired look.

4. Apply wood glue to bottom of 4x4. Place 9" wooden square over glue and secure with screw to create candleholder. Let dry. Repeat for remaining 4x4 and baluster.

5. Using metal shears, cut a tin piece to approx-imately 6" square. Center tin square on top of candleholder and secure with nails. Repeat for remaining candleholders.

6. Cut decorative designs or geometric shapes into tin edges and fold over or up as desired. Edges cut like fringe can be bent over a dowel to create a curled look. (Note: If edges over 1" are folded down, nail to wood.) Repeat for remaining candleholders.

7. Place candles or other decorative objects on top of candleholders.

Candleholders can be made from almost anything. Look at each object you see and try to imagine how to use it as a candleholder. Plates, bowls, serving platters, ashtrays, tiles, and even flat rocks can be placed under candles. As shown on pages 38 and 62, discarded lamps of every style and size can be dismantled and have candles placed inside. Glasses, vases, pitchers, cups, and glass jars can all be filled with deco-rative rocks, beach glass, or marbles and become a new decorative candleholder. As shown on the facing page, even old balusters and weathered pieces of scrap lumber can have candles placed on top.

Candles have become a very important part of decorating, both on the inside of the home and the outside.

On the inside they are used mostly for scent and atmosphere. On the outside they are used for more practical reasons. If used properly, citronella candles can make an evening spent out-of-doors much more pleasant by discour-aging mosquitoes from taking over the area. They not only add ambience through their glow, but also cast light where it may be needed for safety.

Fashionable
accents

A garden is a sacred place where a gardener and those close to him or her can escape the hustle and bustle of modern-day life. Here, one can read a book, write in a journal, celebrate the wonders of nature, or simply relax.

There are many ways a gardener can make his or her piece of earth truly inspirational. Passions, hobbies, and other individual attributes cannot be silenced if the spirit of the gardener is to be given free reign. After all, a garden is a portrait of the gardener.

Birdbaths and statuettes play an integral role in the garden's overall ambience. By purposefully selecting and displaying birdbaths and statuettes, the gardener's personality comes out like the sun. A graceful birdbath can be adorned with faux birds to achieve the illusion of constant companionship. A weathered cherub praying silently beside ankle-high ground covering bestows peace upon all who walk by.

For a very personal and sometimes spiritual touch, a decorative box full of precious artifacts can be attached to a protected place on the outside of the house near any entry. In the box pictured, spiritual and religious keepsakes are exhibited to offer blessings to all who enter or leave.

Facing page: The garden art pictured in these photos are pieces that are usually purchased to be placed indoors. By using each on a covered patio or porch, a delicate touch can be added to a place that is usually reserved for less fragile pieces. Old stained-glass windows, wind chimes made from mosaic pieces of vintage china, hanging lights created from seashells, and a collection of old buoys all add an unexpected style of the gardener who loves to sit on this porch reading the morning paper, enjoying afternoon tea and homemade biscuits, or watching the stars on warm summer evenings.

Upper left: While small hanging crystal lamps are usually restricted to behind closed doors, bringing them out-of-doors is an elegant and wondrous change. This one has been converted to a bird feeder by adding seeds for flying friends.

Lower left: Wind chimes made from broken pieces of china and old silver are made by Becky Edwards, an artist who resides in Idaho and who makes magical things from found objects, mosaics, and copper foil.

Upper right: Small garden statues can be placed anywhere and will fit right in. This one sits on a stacked-stone wall and greets all who come up the long driveway. She is nestled among the greenery and plant life along the wall, so you must notice everything around you or she might be missed.

Porch swings are as traditional as homemade apple pie, and when we close our eyes and visualize a porch on the front of a old country home, the swing is almost always unadorned. Why not cover it with pillows that are washable and inexpensive? Why not make it look like more than you remember?

The swing pictured here was newly purchased and is more traditional. One, however, might want to consider making a swing from an old iron bench. Simply unscrew the legs and add chains to the front and back of each side. Swings can also be made from wooden benches in much the same manner. If you have an old headboard or piece of ironwork that you love,

attach it as a back to a wooden seat, place decorative hooks in the seat, attach chains, and hang it from porch or tree. There are so many ways to make and embellish the traditional porch swing. Paint it pastel, paint it bright bold colors and add floral-print pillows, paint it with faded shabby-chic roses and add vintage chenille throws. You can even faux-finish the back and seat, or decoupage a floral print to the solid back and bench.

With a little imagination and even less time, you can make a piece for patio or garden that will be used over and over and remembered like grandma and her apple pie. It is the porch swing for the grandchildren of today.

Crystal seems like the perfect but often neglected choice when decorating the patio or the porch. It is beautiful both day and night because, whether it be sunlight or candlelight, the reflection of the crystals magnifies the warmth and welcome of a home and its inhabitants.

The candleholders used on this page are all old lamps that were purchased at second-hand stores. The electrical parts and wiring were removed, the glass and any other parts that were considered unattractive were disposed of, and the metal was cleaned or repainted. Candles were added and the decorations were unusual and beautiful.

Special care should be taken in the selection and arrangement of decorative objects on a porch. The overall mood that a porch radiates is governed by color, manipulation of light and shade, and accessories. Every detail plays a role in the porch's personality.

First of all, the gardener generates ideas to help perpetuate his or her needs and desires for the porch setting. As discussed previously, a porch should be friendly and inviting, it should continue the style of the home, and complement personal life-styles. For instance, for a person whose home and garden is top priority, a porch that shows hours of detail work and elegance is fitting.

Next, the gardener must analyze what he or she desires to emphasize. Is it the beauty of freshly picked flowers? Is it the intricate handiwork of wooden pillars or balusters? Or are the gardener's collectibles a main focus? Does the gardener wish to spotlight the imaginative piecing together of old and new, ornate and simple, or elegant and down-to-earth?

After the gardener selects porch furnishings and decorations, some experimentation might be necessary in order to find just the right arrangement. Consider the impact of grouping objects versus spacing them apart. Ornaments gain prominence when grouped, while spacing dilutes their impact. Asymmetrical balance creates a casual feel, whereas symmetrical balance appears more formal. Sometimes, purposefully leaving a space empty makes a greater impact than decorating it.

When the porch is finally decorated to the gardener's tastes and wishes, it will be a joy in which to relax, entertain, work, or play.

The vibrant colors of the summer sun oftentimes encourage garden designers to re-create the warmth and intensity of the season in their outdoor décor. Here the reds, oranges, and yellows of hot summer afternoons dictate the color scheme of a Bohemian-style garden porch. Combined with these colors, ideas borrowed from the far corners of the globe not only continue the theme, but soften and adorn it so that it is as comfortable as it is exotic.

project
WEATHERED
TABLE

Such exotic details as those shown on the facing page are easily created with practical components that, when placed elsewhere with other items, are as traditional as black wrought-iron garden furniture.

This simple weathered table is a discarded plank picnic table that was painted red and distressed. The chairs, found at a garage sale, were painted with touches of faux finishes and simply recovered in a variety of leftover, mismatched floral prints.

Note: The table used here was old and weathered. If your table is new, you can stain it to create a weathered look.

Instructions

1. Paint table desired color. Let dry 4–6 hours.

2. Following wood grain, sand table randomly to distress and remove paint in desired areas.

The tiny details included in this setting are essential to the overall effect of such a bold decorating scheme. The oversized, brightly colored silk umbrella is easily adorned with purchased tassels that hang randomly around the umbrella's edge. Miniature hanging vases, which at night can be used as votive candle-holders, are tied to the wooden slats that support the umbrella.

The table decorations are changed as easily as the paper plates. Here, stacked woven boxes were borrowed from a guest room inside the house, and placed around the center pole. To honor the special guests, childhood pictures were placed in paper frames and added to the display of boxes.

When considering how to decorate for the summer season or a special occasion, it is not mandatory to use expensive items, to make each item match the theme exactly, or to use only those items designed specifically for outdoor use.

project
HANGING CANDLE LAMPS

Materials
Assorted beads
Beading wire
Brass ring(s) 1" (2)
Candle(s) (1–2)
Chain 36"–48"
Copper sheeting
Glass bowl(s) from light
fixture (1–2)
Hook(s) (1–2)
Tape

Supplies
Metal shears
Needle
Needle-nosed pliers
Tape measure
Wire cutters

Candle Lamp #1

Instructions for Candle Lamp #1

1. Cut a piece of wire approximately 40" long. Secure wire by wrapping around once under rim of glass bowl. Tightly twist end of wire to remaining length, or "free-end."

2. String a bead onto free-end of wire. Bring up to rim and thread under, then over, wire that was just secured to rim to form a small loop. Repeat until free-end has been looped completely around circumference of bowl (with a bead hanging from bottom of each loop). See Diagram A on page 69.

3. When first row has been completed, start new row by stringing a bead and looping free-end under, then over, bottom of each loop previously created (where beads hang). Repeat until second row has been completed. See Diagram B on page 69.

4. Start new row and repeat as above, cutting and attaching new length of wire if necessary. Continue beading entire glass bowl. Secure wire by twisting free-end to last loop on last row.

5. Cut a piece of chain to fit tightly under rim of glass bowl and secure. Cut remaining chain into three equal lengths. Evenly space and attach chains under rim to create candle lamp.

6. Place candle in candle lamp.

7. Attach opposite ends of chains to brass ring and hang from hook.

Diagram A

Diagram B

Instructions for Candle Lamp #2

1. Cut a piece of wire approximately 5" long. String beads on wire. Form a circle with beaded wire and secure by twisting ends together. Place underneath glass bowl.

2. Cut six pieces of wire approximately 14" long. Evenly space and attach wires to beaded circle by twisting wire ends in between beads. String assorted beads on wires up to rim of glass bowl.

3. Cut a ½"-wide strip of copper sheeting with metal shears long enough to fit around rim of glass bowl and overlap by 1". Hold in place with tape.

4. Pierce two holes vertically with needle, approximately ¼" apart, in overlapping ends of copper sheeting. Thread beaded wire in through bottom hole in copper sheeting, and out through top hole. Repeat for all wires, spacing evenly. Remove tape.

5. String assorted beads approximately 5" up each wire. Secure by twisting ends of wires around brass ring to create candle lamp.

6. Place candle in candle lamp.

7. Hang by brass ring, or cut a piece of wire to desired length and secure to brass ring for hanging.

Candle Lamp #2

69

project
RUSTED
LAMP STANDS

Materials	*Supplies*
Ceramic lamp	Paper towels
Clear sealant (optional)	Sandpaper
Liquid ground iron	Sponge brushes (2)
Rusting agent	Wire cutters

How to Disassemble Table Lamp

1. Make certain lamp is not plugged into electrical outlet.

2. Using wire cutters, cut off electrical cord at base of lamp.

3. Unscrew bolt at base of lamp. Unscrew light bulb socket and pull out electrical cord through lamp at top.

Note: If lamp is made of more than one piece, the pieces will come apart as the rod that holds them together is removed with the light bulb socket.

Instructions

1. Disassemble lamp and discard all electrical parts, following How to Disassemble Table Lamp directions.

2. Sand lamp stand to roughen up surface. Wipe off dust with damp paper towel. Let dry.

3. Using sponge brush, apply one coat of liquid ground iron to lamp stand, following manufac-

turer's directions. Let dry, and apply a second coat. Let dry 24 hours. Dispose of sponge brush.

4. Using sponge brush, apply one coat of rusting agent to lamp stand, following manufacturer's directions. Let dry. Additional coats of rusting agent may be applied to achieve desired look. Let each coat dry thoroughly before applying additional coats.

5. If desired, apply sealant 48–72 hours after last coat of rusting agent has been applied. (Note: Sealant may change texture of lamp stand.)

6. Reassemble lamp stand, then top with rusted iron finials or other decorative pieces.

Once discarded, old wooden alters, or "niches," can be sponge-painted, using leftover house paints and following the easy step-by-step directions found in any beginner book on faux-finishing. Make certain to seal with a deck sealer or outdoor varnish. Place these in the garden to house delicate flowers or plants, handmade garden vases, or hand-painted pots. Look for these unusual shapes in junk or salvage stores. They are sometimes pieces broken from a fireplace mantle or a large armoire that the owner considered no longer useful.

Facing page: If you do not have time to reupholster a chair for everyday outdoor use or a special garden party, simply purchase a beach-sized towel and a small pillow, and throw it over the back of any kitchen or patio chair.

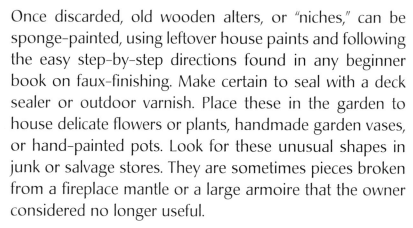

74

Outdoor arrangements can consist of any number of items in any number of combinations. In the photo at the left, a large number of candleholders cover the top of a table to offer light to a dark corner of the garden. Placed not too far from a favorite garden spot that is frequented by almost every visitor, this adds an additional dramatic essence to the garden.

Below, a traditional arrangement that might be found in any living room has been placed on a dining buffet that is now on the covered patio in the garden. The items placed here can be strictly for decoration or can be those that will be used during parties and celebrations.

Garden arrangements can be identical, can contain items that are the same but different, or can be an eclectic accumulation of odds and ends. They can be used every day during the summer, displayed only on certain occasions, or for holidays.

On the facing page, far left column, three ideas for combining items to display during different celebrated seasons are shown. On the stairs at the lower left are three candleholders that are very much the same, yet different. Each is made from purchased metal candlesticks and candles; however, each has a different metal "shade." The shades were made by taking out the glass and electrical parts from old Mexican lamps. This technique is similar to the one discussed on page 38.

Clever concepts

There is no place like a garden to rejuvenate yet calm the soul. Because no two souls are alike, it is only natural that no two gardens are alike. Each gardener wants to cultivate uniqueness in his or her piece of earth. He or she wants to use unexpected elements that have meaning and memories to create a personal garden that is like no one else's.

The photos on this page show how, in different gardens, in different parts of the country, gardeners decorate with what they love most. On a country road in the east, an old barn has been decorated with discarded license plates and small metal signs. For some, such a display would not be considered garden art; but to this gardener, each of these pieces brings back memories of places traveled and special occasions spent far from home.

The yellow wooden shoes from Holland could be considered the same style of garden art as the license plates. These were purchased on a trip by this gardener; and each time he sees them, placed among the spring flowers, they become an album filled with photographs to him.

This old iron bed, once owned by a grandmother, was given to her granddaughter who simply did not have a place in her home for it. Because it was a gift from someone very special, she placed it in her garden. It is here that when the grandmother comes to visit they work a little, have tea, and share precious moments together.

These plant stakes were made by Susan Alexander and Taffnie Bogart for the small garden boxes that surround their studio and their homes. These are made from ceramics, which is a medium they both love and use as a part of their livelihood. If as a gardener, you do not make ceramic pieces of your own, consider different kinds of items than are usual garden décor to place among your flowers.

The display of birdhouses on the facing page is a more traditional garden ornament, but they each have significant value to the gardener who tends this natural garden space.

The decorations or art in the garden, like those inside the home, should happen over time. Of course, you can make a conscious effort to frequent local garden centers to purchase items as quickly as possible, just as some do by hiring a decorator and buying all of their furnishings at the same time. Where is the pleasure in this method of collecting garden art? Where is the thrill of the hunt? Where is the anticipation of finding the perfect piece for the perfect place? It is more economical, and much more fun to wait for just the right piece of garden art to come along–on a trip, at a Saturday afternoon garage sale, or received as a gift. Always leave room, and maybe even plan ahead, for one more unexpected find. Plan for a focal point in your rose garden, even though you have yet to find the perfect birdbath to place in the center. Place a large pot of flowers in a perennial bed of sunflowers as a space holder until you find the perfect birdhouse. Plant an area of greenery to act as a backdrop for a statue of a garden angel that you have yet to find. By the time you locate her, the greenery will have grown into place and will become the perfect backdrop.

All garden art has a job to do, from delighting the eye to giving shape or focus to the garden. However, some pieces of garden art participate more actively than others in everyday garden life. Some cater to wildlife or coddle new transplants. While others offer a new home and sustenance to small animals. Some art comes to the garden to fulfill a need, and to remain as an integral part of the garden's existence.

The birdhouses on these two pages are just such essential honored guests in any garden. A bird feeder, regardless of how it is designed or decorated, is inseparable from the birds it supplies with seed throughout the year; its form alone has come to represent their feathered charm.

If you want to ensure tenants will come to their new homes, keep the following features in mind: 1. Ample room: different birds prefer different sizes of nests and entry holes. 2. Welcome mat: a rough patch below the entry hole—inside and out—helps the birds to come and go. 3. Adequate shelter: a steeply pitched roof with ample overhang will help keep the rain out, while holes drilled in the floor allows moisture to drain. 4. Proper air: a birdhouse must have vents or holes drilled beneath the roof overhang. 5. Maid service: A hinged or removable roof or sides allows easy access for cleaning once the birds have left the nest for the season.

Birdhouses have become very popular for both inside and outside décor. They are fun to buy, easy to decorate or make from scratch, a pleasure to arrange and rearrange in any garden setting, as well as being a valued offering to feathered friends. If you do not have the skills or the time to make a birdhouse from scratch, buy a preassembled birdhouse. Paint it the colors you love and add accents that range from realistic to fanciful. The birdhouse pictured at the left was decorated by an artist from Seattle. It has tiny rocks to resemble a chimney and a wall; it has a tree placed strategically so that it will blend in naturally with the environment; and it has a tiny sign that reads, "Birdance Ranch." The birdhouse pictured at bottom-center is a primitively built box that was decoupaged with art work. The simple hand-painted "tongue-in-cheek" bird feeder at bottom-right is one owned by a gardener who loves her cats as much as her garden and the plants and animals who live there.

Admittedly, some decorations like those pictured on this page are not for every garden or every gardener. A weary wagon wheel resting against the side of the house works better for a country dwelling than a metropolitan condo. As shown in the top photograph, a rusted washbasin makes a fresh ornament amongst wild-flowers. The dried wreath hung on the outside shutters offers feed for the birds as well as casual charm. An old head-board and footboard, as shown in the lower left photograph, emerges from the freshly turned earth. A cleverly placed tea tray brings a fresh approach to "breakfast in bed." An old picket fence makes a back-drop for a planter box, an old wagon is soon to become a garden in itself, and the statue at the right stands quietly alone.

Behind each garden gate lies a new world, unexplored and unknown. Yet step inside and you will find familiar landmarks. Distinctive pieces of garden art let the visitor know where they are, what the gardener loves, and what other surprises might be just down the path.

Any ornament is a type of sign language. Without a word being said, it can set a tone, establish a style, and sometimes reveal the garden's geographic and cultural roots. Sometimes such ornament selection and placement happens naturally without thought, and sometimes it is done with a deliberate consciousness.

Any garden art is acceptable if it is loved by the garden and the gardener, but because your house is in essence the largest garden ornament

you have, it should not be ignored when choosing the art that surrounds it. Childhood years lived somewhere else, mementos from distant travels, and visits to faraway gardens can offer adornments and provide inspiration, but use caution. A marble Venus may look appropriate in an Italian garden but garish and funeral-like in a small garden in Chicago. Or a Japanese tea garden is peaceful and inviting in the northeast, but bizarrely out of place in a cactus garden in the Arizona desert.

However, with common sense and a hint of caution in mind, why stick to the expected garden ornaments? Even if you do live in a distinct geographical location, you may not want your garden to resemble every other garden in the area.

Left: This gardener in Utah loves old things, and because her home was built in 1929, she has used many vintage pieces in her garden. This silver tea service was purchased on a Saturday afternoon in Soho, brought home, and turned into a row of essential garden art. They are strategically placed as hose guards, but some double as bird feeders and candle-holders. (The metal posts were welded to the bottom of the individual pieces by a professional welder.)

The top photograph on this page indicates that this gardener is not only imaginative but frugal. She is one who hates to throw away or waste anything; so here, broken pots were arranged with flowers and shrubs to become an enchanting piece of garden art.

The photograph at the bottom right tells a story of a kind heart, a fondness for travel, a love of vintage anything and everything, and a great individual sense of placement and detail. An old suitcase painted with clear deck sealer is used as the base for part of this display. Some of the plants are placed in old fondue pots and copper chaffing dishes that were purchased from second-hand stores. A 1950's ceramic lamp base has become a candlestand for a large round citronella candle.

Whether gardening is merely a hobby, or a definite lifeline, most gardeners find that a solarium is necessary for nurturing fragile seedlings or exposing established plants to warm, therapeutic sunlight. However, not everyone's home or porch has a beautiful glass-enclosed, English-style solarium. This smaller rendition, made from an old window that was painted to match the pots, is one that can be as functional as it is charming.

The advantage to having a smaller greenhouse such as this one is that it can be moved around in the garden where it is needed.

project
SOLARIUM

Materials
Acrylic paints,
desired colors (2)
Cedar fencing material
½" x 6" x enough length
to accommodate all
four sides of window
Corner brackets
2" x 2" (4)
Hinges 2" (2)
Window frame with glass
Wood screws

Supplies
Drill and bit
Sandpaper
Saw
Sponge brushes (2)
Tape measure

Note: Wood can be cut to specifications at your local lumberyard. The solarium shown was painted in pieces. The pieces were first painted blue, then painted again with pink. Once dry, the pieces were distressed with sandpaper to show some blue.

Instructions

1. Measure height and width of window. Cut two pieces of fencing material to each dimension for box frame. (Note: Window shown overlaps box frame by approximately 1").

2. Assemble box frame, using drill, wood screws, and corner brackets.

3. Paint box frame and window frame with first color and let dry.

4. Paint box frame and window frame with second color and let dry.

5. Sand box frame and window frame to distress and show first color of paint in desired areas.

6. Attach window to box frame, using drill, wood screws, and hinges.

Wooden screens are typically used indoors as closet doors, window shutters, room dividers, backdrops, or dressing screens. Today, however, they have gained popularity as more decorative props, such as photo holders. By taking a wooden screen outdoors, an unexpected element is transformed into gratifying garden art. As shown in the above photograph, seed packets are tucked between the slots. Standard gardening tools, prettied up with small bows, hang at varying heights along the screen. During the winter and spring months, the packets are removed but the screen is left to weather in the elements.

Any porch or garden area is more enjoyable for all who visit there if plenty of potted plants are in attendance. Banish boredom by displaying potted flowers and plants in atypical containers and in original ways. At the left, spanish terra-cotta tiles were glued to a plain wooden box. An easy faux finish was applied, with a heavy-duty outdoor sealer as the final coat. This gardener now has a wonderful new piece of garden art.

Once you begin looking at the pieces in your garden as art, it will be difficult to include plain traditional garden pieces amidst the natural beauty of the flowers and trees. No longer is a pot placed alone on top of a garden wall—a discarded wicker chair is added as well to give detail. An unfinished terra-cotta pot can be wrapped in lace, spray-painted, and then after the lace is removed, placed among the ivy cascading over the rocks.

86

project
FORK
FENCE

Materials
19-gauge wire
Clay pots (3–4)
Exterior paint, white
Golden oak spray stain
Old meat forks
(one for each pot)
Picket fence section
Plants
Potting soil

Supplies
Flat paintbrush
approximately 2"
Pliers
Tape measure
Wire cutters

Instructions

1. Paint fence section white. Let dry 24 hours.

2. Spray fence section with stain, following manufacturer's directions. Let dry.

3. Measure wire long enough to wrap around pot below rim, add 3" and cut. Form a ring for pot by wrapping wire under rim and tightly twisting ends together. Cut away any excess wire. Remove ring from pot.

4. Measure another piece of wire to desired handle length, add 3" and cut. Secure one end of wire to ring and secure opposite end of wire to opposite side of ring to form a handle. Slip pot into ring and set aside.

5. Using pliers, bend fork tines up toward handle.

6. Measure wire long enough to wrap around fence slat and fork handle. Secure forks to fence slat, twisting wire ends together in back. Cut away any excess wire.

7. Fill pots with soil and desired plants and hang on fork tines.

Cooks, collectors, gardeners, what else? This cook-collector-gardener attached her old kitchen utensils to a whitewashed section of garden fence and made a decorative piece to hold hanging pots under her kitchen window.

project
TULIP CANDLE-HOLDER

Materials
Candle
Candleholder
Colored marker,
desired color
Metal rod ¼" diameter,
36" long
Metal sheeting
Paper
Pencil
Solder
Spray paints, desired colors

Supplies
Metal shears
Pliers
Scissors
Soldering iron

Note: The tulip candleholder shown was painted pink for the petals, and green for the leaves.

Instructions

1. Using pencil, draw a tulip petal pattern onto paper, making petal width ½ the circumference of candleholder. Draw a tulip leaf pattern. Cut out patterns.

2. Using marker and patterns, trace three petal shapes onto sheeting. Trace two leaf shapes. Using metal shears, cut out shapes.

3. Using pliers, bend petal shapes into a curve and assemble into tulip shape with edges overlapping.

4. Solder petals together at bottom.

5. Spray-paint petals and leaves, following manufacturer's directions, and let dry.

6. Insert rod at center of tulip bottom and solder.

7. Solder two leaves onto rod below tulip bottom.

8. Bend petals and leaves slightly back at top.

9. Place candle and candleholder in tulip.

It is true that garden art should usually be geographically and historically correct, but sometimes, for fun, maybe it doesn't need to be.

The gardener who owns the gourd bird feeder at the left does not live in the country where gourds are grown and easily found. She lives in a big city complex where most decorations are are made from contemporary man-made materials. However, she found this gourd on a trip to the mountains of the west, and loves to see it hanging outside her back door. It brings a breath of fresh country air to a somewhat polluted environment.

The owner of the garden pictured at the right, lives at the foot of the Rocky Mountains, but loves the ocean almost as much as she does the rugged grandeur of the west. During one very special vacation, shells and weathered candlesticks were collected; and they hold far too many memories to have them stored away. So, for a few summer months, they are placed in a quiet corner of the garden—where she is certain she can smell the ocean breeze.

project GOURD BIRD FEEDER

Materials
Bird seed
Dried gourd,
deep bowl shape
Twisted twine

Supplies
Craft knife
Drill and ¹⁄₁₆" bit
Pencil
Small hand saw

Instructions

1. Using hand saw, cut off neck of gourd to create a bowl. Clean out seeds and plant material.

2. Draw desired pattern on outside of gourd.

3. Using craft knife, carve pattern in surface of gourd, and drill small holes in pattern for birds to feed.

4. Drill holes on opposite sides at top of gourd.

5. Cut length of twine approximately 36" long and thread each end into holes at top of gourd. Tie twine ends into knots inside gourd.

6. Hang and fill with birdseed.

project
BALUSTER
CANDLE-
STICKS

Instructions

1. Saw balusters to desired heights, varying heights for visual impact. Level bottoms of balusters so they will stand.

2. Drill a hole for candle cups in top center of each baluster to create candlesticks.

3. Place candle cups in drilled holes.

4. Place taper candles in candle cups.

Materials	*Supplies*
Candle cups (3)	Drill and ¾"
Old balusters (3)	spade bit
Taper candles (3)	Scroll saw

Certain pieces of handmade art have special meaning to those who create them and often to those who buy them. Sometimes pieces of art are purchased simply for their beauty and the emotions they elicit personally—not for their universal significance and intent. This is true of this piece of art. The owner does not believe that it was intended to be put outdoors in the garden. The designer explained the symbolism of this piece to the owner, but she can't remember. All she knows is that she loves it, so she made several pieces of her own that look like it. Each is placed strategically in her garden. Guardian or mischief maker—it is hard to tell. However, it cannot be denied that this tiny piece of garden art has cast a powerful spell and has meaning to the owner.

The wide variety of plant stakes that are pictured on the facing page have no significant meanings—they are simply a form of decoration. Some are ceramic pieces and some are painted wood—but all can be purchased or easily made. They are perfect to add to all of the plants in your garden or give as gifts for your friend's garden.

When selecting items for plant stakes, use your imagination. How about a tall skinny candleholder with a candle to light during the evening hours? Or consider a china teacup and saucer, glued to a copper pipe, that holds birdseed?

project
GARDEN
VASES

Materials	*Supplies*
Cylinder bud vase(s)	Flat paintbrush
Glass conditioner	New pencil with
Glass paints, desired color(s)	flat eraser
Plant support stake(s)	Small, pointed
	paintbrush
	Sponge brush
	Transparent tape

Instructions

1. Wash vase and dry thoroughly.

2. Using sponge brush, apply one coat of glass conditioner to vase, following manufacturer's directions. Let dry.

3. Paint vase(s) using desired Painting Technique(s) on facing page and let dry.

4. Place vase(s) in plant support stake(s).

What most artists do when they begin to create is look around them and see what they have that is intended for one use, yet can be used for something else. That is just what this gardener/artist did when she took these bud vases, painted them with brightly colored paints, and placed them in purchased plant support stakes. They are now garden vases and add a touch of color to an all-green garden—plus they make everyday look like fresh cut flowers have just been delivered for a party.

Painting Techniques

1. Stripes: Apply transparent tape to vase horizontally or vertically, leaving a space between pieces for desired width of stripe. Smooth any air bubbles or gaps with fingers when applying to ensure that paint will not seep underneath tape. Using flat paintbrush and desired color of paint, paint between pieces of tape. Paint two coats if necessary. Let dry. Remove tape.

2. Spiral: Apply transparent tape, spiraling upward or downward, the length of vase. Smooth tape and apply paint as in Technique 1.

Diagram B

3. Polka Dots: Dip pencil eraser in paint of desired color and press lightly on vase to create a small dot. Apply dots at random. Set aside and let dry. See Diagram A.

4. Daisies: Dip bristles of pointed paintbrush in paint of desired color. Applying a small amount of pressure, lay brush tip partially down on vase, making a raindrop shape to form a daisy petal. Repeat until each daisy has at least five petals. Dip handle end of pointed paintbrush in paint of a contrasting color and dot center of each daisy.

See Diagram B. Create leaves below petals with same technique, if desired.

Diagram C

5. Swirls: Dip bristles of pointed paintbrush in paint of desired color. Paint small swirls on vase. Repeat in a random pattern for desired look. See Diagram C.

The garden art on this and the preceding pages reflects how the past finds a future. Hunted for in attics, garages, and sheds, some of the decorations shown here are family castoffs and some are family heirlooms.

Flowers can be planted and contained in a variety of objects—from a hand-decorated terra-cotta pot to an antique wheelbarrow. What could be more charming than a baby carriage frame filled with everblooming miniature blossoms, or an old delivery tricycle adorned with a duo of flowering baskets?

For a more masculine look, perch a metal sculpture, such as the sphere pictured on the upper left, on an old tree stump. It is enough to change any flower or vegetable garden into a field of dreams.

There are other items, not pictured here, that might be of interest to the men in your family—they might even spend more time in the garden. They oftentimes like decorative pieces carved from wood, or furniture that is more massive in nature and made structurally sound from familiar materials.

For a more feminine look, take the legs from an antique sewing machine, wrap a pot in burlap to hide the container, and stand it at the beginning of your garden path. It will be a beautiful welcome to all who pay you a visit. If burlap is not your choice of fabrics, choose one that can withstand the dripping water from the pot and will not fade in the sun.

It is the little details that give a garden a signature look. For example, see how in the photograph to the left, a dime-store hanging basket filled with fresh daisies makes an otherwise ordinary garden fence a place to stop and notice.

Or, as shown in the center picture, one can pair function with beauty by leaving a watering can beside the geranium it sprinkles. Notice that the flower box is made from an old wooden box and a discarded stair baluster. In the picture just below, a distressed wooden chair keeps a flower garden company—a delightful sight in a sunflower-splashed garden.

On the facing page, fairy-tale charm was nonchalantly created by leaning a straw broom against the back door. It brings to mind the stories told to us as children. The ceramic jug nestled beside it adds to the simplicity of the "picture" and yet tells a story of its own.

Whether handy to use or simply nice to look at, these dainty details bring charm to any corner or area of the garden that needs a lift.

Piece by piece

Substantial pieces of art, meticulously selected and placed, improve the appearance of virtually any garden. Line a garden pathway with a single elaborate and voluminous urn, and marvel at the masterpiece before your eyes. A sacred crucifix sculpture makes visitors keenly aware of the mind-body-soul connection a breathtaking garden inspires. There can be many of these single pieces in your garden, but for most of us, they are added one at a time, as time and money may allow. In the end, these pieces are those that collectively decorate the garden.

Garden art need not be simply decorative in nature—it can be functional as well. Here to the left, in the middle of a field is a luncheon table that is kept set for daily lunches for the gardener and his or her friends. If you are not so fortunate as to have a field in your backyard, a small clearing carpeted in crunchy, warm-hued leaves is all that you need to present your own interpretation of this lovely scene. This garden lunch could be considered complete at any time, yet it is the perfect place to add a new detail on an almost daily basis. The quaint wooden chair, the floral tablecloth, the checked napkins, and the simple floral centerpiece—it is obvious that this backyard café was brought together with amour. The addition of a bottle of wine and two crystal wine glasses could render the atmosphere in this garden hopelessly romantic.

In the garden below, the gardener adds favorite pieces of china as she breaks them or finds them in favorite second-hand stores. Look closely at the plates that line the birdbath or act as a border for the planter box. Fragile dishes are not predictable garden accents, but if they are chipped and broken, and the area is protected, they add a wonderfully delicate accent.

project TWIG TOPIARY

Materials
Branches, at least 48" long and
1" diameter at one end (2)
Floral wire
Large flowerpot, containing
soil and desired climbing plant
Twigs or vines (3–5)

Instructions

1. Anchor larger end of branches at opposite sides inside flowerpot.

2. Arch branches toward each other and bend to form a wreath shape. Wire all ends to secure.

3. Weave twigs or vines in wreath.

4. Train climbing plant to grow up sides of wreath to create topiary.

The one thing about loving your garden art is that you usually cannot leave anything alone to be ordinary or traditional. Every detail must be perfect and unexpected. Which is oftentimes true with details that are eventually covered up. A perfect example of this is topiaries and trellises. Some are wooden or metal and are plain utilitarian pieces; others can be ornate or magnificent in their simplicity. The topiaries and trellises pictured in this book are made from natural materials. They add that special touch to the garden and the growing plants without being too noticeable or too unusual.

When building a topiary support or trellis make certain that it is large enough and strong enough to support the plants that will be growing up its form. If you misjudge how heavy the plant will be at full growth, and the weight of it destroys the support, you may have to dig up the plant to remove the broken pieces. Also, if it is placed against a wall, make certain that wooden spacer blocks are attached first, so the vines have room to wrap between the supports and the wall without being damaged.

Less is more. This is a popular school of thought for modern interior decorating and it can be replicated outdoors as well. This, afterall, is the generation that is practicing simple abundance—for everything you add, you must take something away. It is true, for all of us, however, that a simple decoration can truly have a groundbreaking effect. Try to picture the top photograph without the geranium on the bench and then ask yourself, "Is it as inviting?" "Is it as beautiful?"

This philosophy could be considered the cornerstone for *Two-Hour Garden Art*. It is possible to make your garden much more appealing, with a small, simple touch that can be made or added in a short period of time.

Now imagine the same bench covered with all types of decorations—statuettes, vases, birdhouses, potted flowers galore—and ask yourself the same two questions. If it is this version that you enjoy the most, it can still be accomplished in short periods of time. Try adding one new item each day, or allocating just two hours maybe first thing in the morning, for making and discovering new objects.

The orientally inspired pot pond at the right is one of these types of projects. It can be made elegantly and very simply in a Japanese-style pot with a few rocks and a floating lily, and it can have any unusual items added as they are discovered.

project
MOSAIC
POT

Materials	*Supplies*
Acrylic spray varnish	Putty knife
Clay pot	Utility sponge
Premixed grout	
Seashells	

Instructions

1. Using putty knife, apply grout approximately ¼" thick to outside of pot. Thickness of grout is determined by size of seashells used.

2. Press seashells into grout until entire pot is covered. You may reposition shells while grout is still wet.

3. Using damp sponge, wipe off excess grout from seashells and let dry.

4. Spray pot with varnish, following manufacturer's directions, and let dry.

Mosaics are a well-loved art form that are gaining a renewed popularity among almost every area of art today. A mosaic can be made from shells—as shown in this photo—or cuts of colored glass, pieces of broken ceramics, bottle caps, stones, or any other small or broken material. Traditionally, the pieces used to create a mosaic form a picture or a pattern. Also, it is customary to use pieces of the same, or similar, material. As with any art, straying from the norm can result in an entirely new and creative definition.

111

MOSAIC STEPPING-STONES

Materials
Cement
Cement sealer
Cement topping mix
Ceramic ware
Colored glass
Tile pieces

Supplies
Chicken wire
Clean cloth
Cloth gloves
Contact paper
Hammer
Paper towels
Petroleum jelly
Sponge
Stepping-stone mold
Tile cutters
Wire cutters

Instructions

1. Prepare glass by breaking into pieces. Glass and ceramic ware can be safely broken by backing with contact paper and tapping with a hammer. Cut tile with tile cutters.

2. Cut chicken wire to fit inside stepping-stone mold and set aside.

3. Using a clean cloth, coat inside of mold with petroleum jelly.

4. Place glass and tile pieces, color side down, as desired into mold.

5. Mix a moderate amount of cement topping mix, following manufacturer's directions. Pour topping mix over glass pieces until mold is approximately ¼ full. Wearing gloves, smooth to even out.

6. Mix a generous amount of cement, following manufacturer's directions. Pour into mold until ½ full. Wearing gloves, smooth to even out.

7. Lay cut chicken wire over cement. Pour remaining cement over wire. Smooth to even out. Gently tap underside of mold with hammer to work out bubbles.

8. Soak up excess water on surface with paper towels. Repeat until all water has been absorbed.

9. Let cement set. Do not move until completely set. (Note: Quick-set cement will be ready in 2–3 hours; regular cement requires 2 days.)

10. Remove stone from mold when set.

11. Prepare more cement topping mix to fill in any gaps or holes that appear on top. Wipe off topping from glass and tile pieces with a damp sponge.

12. After 30 days, seal with cement sealer.

Small details such as those shown in the photographs on this page can be a delightful touch to any garden. The Pennsylvania Dutch-style painting on the side of this flower box makes it more than just a planter. The bird's nest on top of the garden torch pictured above gives this area of the garden entirely new meaning, such as life, or rebirth.

A bird's nest, whether newly patched together or already abandoned, is such a delightful discovery. Many gardeners have an affinity for nests, perhaps since the bird's nest symbolizes what human families go through in the circle of life. The meticulous preparation before a birth is dubbed "nesting" for both birds and humans alike. Then, the eggs are carefully and lovingly guarded until birth. In no time at all, the babies fly away on their own—hesitant, yet anxious to start a new life, a new nest. What is left is the "empty nest"—a term with which humans are only too familiar .

project
STONE
PLANTERS

Materials
Anchor bolts ½" (4–5)
Mortar mix
Stone or rock planters

Supplies
Drill and
masonry bit

Instructions

1. Predrill ½" holes in side of planter that will be against wall, and corresponding holes in wall where planter is to be placed.

2. Mix mortar, following manufacturer's directions.

3. Apply mortar to drilled side of planter in all places that will be against wall, and into drilled holes in wall.

4. Place planter against wall, making certain to line up holes in planter with holes in wall. Secure in place with anchor bolts. Let mortar set for several days before filling.

project
RUSTED
WALL

Materials	*Supplies*
Exterior paint, terra-cotta orange	Paintbrush or roller
Indoor/outdoor acrylic paints: white, desired colors	Rags (2–3)
	Sponges (2–3)
Oil-based walnut stain	
Old picture frames	
Rusted garden art	

Instructions

1. Paint wall with terra-cotta orange, using paintbrush or roller, and let dry.

2. Sponge on white acrylic paint and rub off gently with rags for desired look.

3. Using rag, apply walnut stain over white paint and rub off gently for desired look.

4. Dip sponges in paints of desired colors and splatter wall or throw sponges at wall. Repeat until desired look is achieved and let dry.

5. Hang old frames on wall and place rusted garden art around wall to add decorative elements.

The wall pictured here mimics in an artsy sort of way the graffiti painted on the walls of subways and industrial buildings in big cities. An eccentric potpourri of garden art sprawled across a sponge-stained backdrop is as provocative as downtown graffiti.

115

Under a Christmas tree, a toy train chugs around a cheerful little village. Welcome back to the land of pretend, where tiny ear-muffed dolls spin figure eights on a mirror pond, and the cotton-spun snowdrifts never melt. A miniature village, just as magical as the one you remember in your yuletide living room or department store window, can be re-created right in your own backyard.

For a gardener who never grew up, for one who never lost his or her fascination with small trains and the images and stories they create, dwarfed villages, as shown on these pages, can bring back many enchanted childhood memories.

Small rocks, real trees and bushes, and natural flowers landscape the village perfectly. The scaled-down buildings, windmill, church, train stop, and various shops and houses are each created with loving care. These of course, are not landscapes that can be created in two hours time, but each tiny section can be. This is a project that could take a lifetime to complete—after all, there is the waterfall to be added, and a train tour through the mountains, and . . .

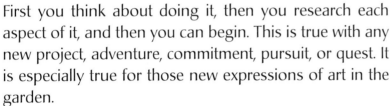

First you think about doing it, then you research each aspect of it, and then you can begin. This is true with any new project, adventure, commitment, pursuit, or quest. It is especially true for those new expressions of art in the garden.

Whether creating something as traditional as a Japanese tea garden, as ambitious as a producing series of orchards, or as imaginative as a backyard miniature village with a working toy train, you must be certain to do your homework. It is essential that you have a clear understanding of all the answers to "Why?" and "Why not?" You should also have a clear understanding and knowledge of the best products and techniques that have already been tested by the experts, and a compre-hensive knowledge of the procedures and details. It is not surprising that tremendous amounts of time, energy and money can be spent, and then spent again if you do not complete the preliminary work and follow the advice of the experts. If your new expression of piece-by-piece garden art is to be enjoyed while it is being created, as well as for years to come, it must first be studied and then carried out.

project
TWIG
TRELLIS

Materials
Branches:
24" length (3)
30" length (2)
36" length (3)
40" length (2)
60" length (4)
Nails 1¼" (1 box)
Wire

Supplies
Hammer

Note: Branches should be straight and approximately 1" in diameter. Trim twigs from side branches.

Instructions

1. Place four 60" branches vertically, approximately 12" apart.

2. Place three 36" branches horizontally across the four 60" pieces to create crossbars. Place first crossbar approximately 12" up from bottom. Place second crossbar approximately 18" up from first. Place third crossbar 12" down from top. Nail branches together at cross sections to create trellis.

3. Twist two 40" branches together lengthwise and nail to secure. Nail each end to top of outer 60" branches to create outermost arch.

4. Twist two 30" branches together lengthwise and nail to secure. Nail each end to top of inner 60" branches to create innermost arch.

5. Nail one 24" branch to top center of outermost arch and nail to center of top crossbar. This will cross center of innermost arch. Nail at cross section of innermost arch.

6. Nail two 24" branches at 45° angles to left and right of first 24" branch, securing opposite end at center of top crossbar next to first 24" branch. Nail at cross sections of innermost arch.

7. Turn trellis over and nail cross sections from behind. Wire cross sections and joining pieces for additional strength.

project
TWIG
CORRAL

Materials   *Supplies*
Branches 2" thick,   Hammer
16" long
Twig and vine cuttings

Note: Start with a flower bed raised with wooden rails or planks.

Instructions

1. Hammer end of branch approximately 2" into ground directly against side of flower bed. Repeat every 36" around entire flower bed.

2. Hammer another branch 2" into ground parallel to first branch approximately 3" out from flower bed. Repeat around entire flower bed to create a trough, making certain to line up with first set of branches.

3. Drop twig and vine cuttings into trough parallel to edge and around entire flower bed.

121

To some, gardens indicate the need for massive elements that will be in the garden for as long as the garden stands. In some cases, these elements can be in their natural state, and sometimes they have an added human touch.

The stone bench above is exactly as it was when it was delivered from the rock quarry. It can be a bench, a means of support, or simply a decorative element.

The rock pictured on the facing page was simply too heavy to move and has been here since the beginning. Because its massive plainness was not what the gardener wished for in the center of his garden, a delicate and useful design was carved into its surface.

As we design, plant, and inevitably tear up and redo our gardens, where do all of our ideas come from? Trial and error, the pages of books, the sights seen while traveling, and from walking along neighborhood streets on warm summer evenings. All give us segments of the inspiration we need to plant and decorate our own gardens. What is it we see and remember in all of these things and places? For each of us it is different and sometimes difficult to explain, or difficult for others to understand. Because everything we see and love is a piece of our own perceptions and experience, what is truly wonderful to one gardener may be offensive to another. The garden art surrounding the house below is perfect for this country gardener and his family. However, for a roof-top garden owned by an aggressive lawyer in the heart of New York City, it would be unwanted and inappropriate. A garden and all that it contains is a personal investment, a personal statement, and a personal triumph. It should be what you want it to be. It should nurture flowers and trees that you want to grow, and arranged in gardens that you love to tend. It should be a place where you can go to retreat from the worries of the day, and find a peace that renews your spirit and calms your soul. It should be a place that shows the possibilities of living and gently takes you through the cycle of life. For some, the time spent in the garden is a spiritual moment in time, filled with small miracles that they can experience on a daily basis, regardless of the month or the year. It is to others, that which brings them closest to what they believe heaven to be.

In garden arrangement, as in all other kinds of decorative work, one has not only to acquire a knowledge of what to do, but also to gain some wisdom in perceiving what it is well to let alone.

—Gertrude Jekyll

In his garden every man may be his own artist without apology or explanation. Here is one spot where each may experience "the romance of possibility."

—Louise Beebe Wilder

125

Metric Equivalency Chart

mm-millimetres   cm-centimetres
inches to millimetres and centimetres

inches	mm	cm	inches	cm	inches	cm
⅛	3	0.3	9	22.9	30	76.2
¼	6	0.6	10	25.4	31	78.7
⅜	10	1.0	11	27.9	32	81.3
½	13	1.3	12	30.5	33	83.8
⅝	16	1.6	13	33.0	34	86.4
¾	19	1.9	14	35.6	35	88.9
⅞	22	2.2	15	38.1	36	91.4
1	25	2.5	16	40.6	37	94.0
1¼	32	3.2	17	43.2	38	96.5
1½	38	3.8	18	45.7	39	99.1
1¾	44	4.4	19	48.3	40	101.6
2	51	5.1	20	50.8	41	104.1
2½	64	6.4	21	53.3	42	106.7
3	76	7.6	22	55.9	43	109.2
3½	89	8.9	23	58.4	44	111.8
4	102	10.2	24	61.0	45	114.3
4½	114	11.4	25	63.5	46	116.8
5	127	12.7	26	66.0	47	119.4
6	152	15.2	27	68.6	48	121.9
7	178	17.8	28	71.1	49	124.5
8	203	20.3	29	73.7	50	127.0

Index

Acknowledgments

We would like to acknowledge and thank the following people for their beneficial contribution to this lovely book.

To the artists who so kindly shared their fabulous pieces with us for use in this book and deserve a heartfelt thanks:

Amy Adams, (Lemonade Stand, pgs 28–35)
Becky Edwards, (Wind-chimes, pg 59–60)
Taffnie Bogart & Susan Alexander (pg 76, & Plant stakes, pg 93 from Handmade Clay Crafts)

To the homeowners who allowed us to photograph their beautiful yards and gardens in which they've sown love and many happy memories:

Amy Adams, Ogden, Utah
Dixie Barber, Park City, Utah
Anita Louise Crane, Park City, Utah
Marni Kissel, Ogden, Utah
Jo Packham, Ogden, Utah
Gene & Carolyn Smith, Ogden, Utah

Sara Toliver, Ogden, Utah

To the photographers and stylists whose attractive work has been added to this book as a part of the beautiful examples of garden art:

Anita Louise Crane: pgs 8, 12, 14 lower-left, 15, 16, 17, 86 center-left & center-right, 87 upper-right, 104, 106, 107, 109, 110, 111

Leslie Newman: pgs 6 upper-left, 14 upper-half, 20, 22 upper-left, 25 lower-left, 27 lower, 67, 80 upper-half & lower-right, 87 left-half, 96 upper-left & right, 98, 100 upper-left & lower-right, 101, 102 lower-right & left, upper-left, 103, 115.

Robert Perron: pgs 22 lower-left, 100 center, 114, 125 center-left & right.

Scot Zimmerman: pgs 7 upper-left, 11 upper-left & lower-right, 13 upper-left & center-right, 77, 80 lower-left, 81, 116, 117, 124.

Hopkinsville-Christian County Public Library
1101 BETHEL STREET
HOPKINSVILLE, KENTUCKY 42240